SWEET SUBMISSION

THIRTY DAYS WALKING WITH GOD IN FAITH, OBEDIENCE, AND PRAYER.

Jennifer A. Lewis

SWEET SUBMISSION

Thirty days walking with God in Faith, Obedience, and Prayer.

Jennifer A. Lewis

ISBN (Print Edition): 978-1-66784-249-3

ISBN (eBook Edition): 978-1-66784-250-9

TABLE OF CONTENTS

INTRODUCTION

When I initially felt led to write this devotional, I hoped to encourage women like myself in their own walks with the Lord. It was a women's thirty-day devotional that had done just that for me when I was in the darkest place and fight of my life. That devotional encouraged me to seek God and stop fighting to keep control in everything I did. It seemed the more I tried to keep control, the less of it I had. My life, relationships, marriage, family, health, jobs … all of it suffered from my desire to keep control. I almost lost it all a time or two by doing it all my own way and not ever God's ways.

So, when I began to write this devotional, I intended to write a 365-day book. I had made up my mind and decided it would be easy. Well, within the ninety days I agreed to give God control of this walk, I began attending a new church. I met new people and got involved with different Bible studies, volunteering in my church and expanding my support system. I was blessed to meet a dear sister in Christ who encouraged me on this book journey, along with diet, health, exercise, and prayer!

During those ninety days, I finished writing 365 days worth of devotionals. I wrote a lot! But I kind of sat still. The enemy came prowling and doubts, worries, and fears crept in, keeping me still. I recognized with gentle prods from the Lord that all of my work was just that: mine. I heard my call, but I went about it my way.

My sweet friend—who I know the Lord placed directly in my path at the time I needed the love, guidance, and prayer—was very persistent in her gentle way. She encouraged me to exercise and eat better. I gave in and joined her workouts and diet program with a commitment to try something new for ninety days. I also started, that very same week, a Bible study, The Battle Plan for Prayer. My friend again reached out to me that first week, with an invitation to a women's ministry retreat. Again I had a million excuses for not going. But I recognized that when God opens a door of opportunity for you, do not slam it shut. I committed to go on the retreat. I started from scratch and began to write again, this time His way. Every day, beginning with Him and ending with Him, recognizing that all of the work I had done previously was of myself, and not that of my Lord.

As the first days passed, with much praying and yes, indeed, even some battles of wills, time came back into play. I felt the Lord scolding me, saying clearly, *Jennifer, I told you to write a book. I didn't tell you to write it in your way or give you a time frame in which I wanted it done.* Those words I heard weighed heavily on my heart. As I prayed, did my daily exercises, planned my meals, and prayed over my Bible study about scheduled prayer, I knew. The ninety-day references were not a coincidence. I was the one who needed the time frame to see whether I would and could commit to doing something for my God. I knew God was using the time frame as His tool, pointing yet again to my control issue. I made a commitment to that, and again he graciously reminded me of just how big He is, beyond space and time. Why was I looking at a time frame for His work to be done? Did I not believe His timing to be perfect? How much time did He, the creator of the universe, need to have me learn the lessons at work? Every answer I came up with was wrong. *Commit, trust, follow, and do* rang like cymbals in my heart. I prayed harder and deeper than I ever had before and I remember saying, "Lord, stop my wants to control this outcome. I will give it to you. I will commit and submit to you, I will trust your ways and your guidance."

Now with two obstacles behind me—or so I thought—the Lord stayed close to me every day. I sought Him in prayer first thing every morning. I worshipped Him and searched His word for exactly what I felt and believed He wanted me to see, learn, and write. Literally, step by step we walked together, and He opened my eyes, my ears, and my heart to the control I had to let Him have. However, I remained dedicated, committed, willing and eager to heed Him. I took each day and each step with faith. And as each obstacle came, I sought His guidance. He led me and took me, step by step:

Step 1: Write a book.

Step 2: Not your way.

Step 3: Not your time.

And just like that, He brought me to day thirty of this walk, and He said, *Jennifer, look what I have done in you and through you these thirty days. Your faith, your obedience, your listening, and your prayer life have all grown, just as if a year has passed! You set limits on me, and what I can and will do! You stayed diligently in my path. You took every step I asked of you. And even in your doubts, you gave me your trust. During the time when you ran ahead, you allowed me to slow you back down, and you learned the reason why you needed to slow down.*

How did my idea of 365 days dwindle to ninety and then to thirty? Well, I believe God wanted me in a specific place at a specific time to teach me to surrender the control I thought I had to have to do His work. He needed me to recognize that, to show me what He can do in His own time. Who am I to question my God? I doubted what He could do, in me and through me. I placed a time frame on how long He would even need to teach it to me. And look at what my God has done!

This thirty days truly has been a collaboration between the Lord and I in complete communication together. Not just in the physical tasks of battling my weaknesses and my health but in the obedience, the faith, and the prayer that was necessary for the walk to even start. I had to commit, persevere, and endure; trust, be willing, and be faithful; pray for His will, His path, and His guidance, diligently with scheduled prayer time and in the spontaneous time when opposition came knocking. He stripped away layers of control from me, making me recognize what I was doing versus what He wanted to do in me. And each new day, we danced in adoration, confession, thanksgiving, and supplication. The walk was beautiful. It is beautiful!

I am not a writer of fancy words. I can't truly describe what He has done for me in this time spent writing and growing, but I earnestly pray that these heartfelt words start a fire deep within you to want to go deeper into a relationship with the Lord, to want to have that very real and personal relationship with Him. I am so excited to see exactly what He can do in His time. It is the sweetest of emotions to submit daily to Him. These thirty days have been just that, a time of sweet submission for me in my walk with Him.

My prayer is that we do this walk together, my sweet friends in Christ. What better way than in prayer together, supplication together, in encouragement of one another, building ourselves in Christ together, relying solely on Him? And on this walk I ask you to commit fully to be in sweet submission to Him, having full faith in His guidance and in daily prayer to do and to allow what He wants done in you. May a transformation of old to new happen. My hope is that this time spent reading what He has done in my life will encourage you, too, in your walk with the Lord.

DAY 1:
WALKING IN FAITH...

OCTOBER 3, 2021

T his early morning, as I started to read my first scriptures and let God speak to me in prayer, my heart and my thoughts ran in ten different directions. *Whew.* Have you ever had so many prayers that you felt needed answers all at one time! Like, right now?

Well, as I bounced around today from Job to Isaiah, from John to Romans, and then from Hebrews to 2 Corinthians, God tied it all into one verse, one of the well-known favorites.

Philippians 4:12-13, "I know what it is to be in need, and I know what it is to have plenty. I have learned the secret of being content in any and every situation, whether well fed or hungry, whether living in plenty or in want. I can do everything through Him who gives me strength."

I can't help but love how the Lord causes me to think deeply about His words, His promises.

How He uses our trials to strengthen our faith in Him.

We sometimes forget or refuse to believe—especially in the midst of our painful trials, or the trials of another—that God does not make mistakes. I know He had to remind me a few times. Sometimes the journey we agree to go on is a hard one! Diet and exercise. Prayer. My health has never been a strong suit for me. It has been a daily struggle these past five-and-a-half years.

God uses our trials to strengthen us and teach us valuable lessons about His faithfulness because He has the power and the wisdom to do so. Because He is all wise and all knowing, He knows from the beginning of a problem to the end of the solution. If our trials served no purpose to God, He simply would not have allowed them to be a part of our human life experience in the first place.

We may not like the way God does things or understand it, but notice He didn't include us in His planning committee before creating the world and the human race. God isn't big on asking you and me for advice. He is, however, big on our asking Him for advice! In fact, I'm sure He feels insulted when we make it a practice not to.

Most folks at some point in their lifetime have this question, one they would love an answer to: "If God is real, why doesn't He show Himself to us?" I can tell you the answer: "Because it would not be wise of Him."

Faith is in what we cannot see …

If we all could see Him in all His glory, power, and might, why, then, would we need faith?

Bottom line, everything God does and allows is wise. At some point, at some time in eternity, that will become abundantly clear to us. Perhaps it would be wise of us to begin believing that at this time. Now.

God uses our struggles to both reveal character flaws and to create Godly character in us …

God loves us too much to just leave us where we are. Our trials all serve a purpose in us, maybe in our family, or even in another person's life. They produce perseverance, hope, and a true reliance on God when we commit to get in the Word. It's food for our daily lives, not just cake to be eaten on special occasions.

Everything is preparation for eternity. Time on earth is short, and eternity is a long time to get this wrong, but with God all things are possible. This is an important fact to remember. If you want to learn more about making it through your worldly trials and burdens, read the Bible and take the first steps of this walk with me.

Job 5:19 Matthew 19:26 John 16:33 Romans 5:3, 8:28-31, 12:12 Isaiah 38:17, 2 Corinthians 12:9 Hebrews 2:10 When we are weak, God is strong!

DAY 2:

A WALK IN HIS COUNSEL ...

OCTOBER 4, 2021

P salm 1:1-3, "Blessed is the man who does not walk in the counsel of the wicked or stand in the way of sinners or sit in the seat of mockers. But his delight is in the law of the Lord, and on his law he meditates day and night. He is like a tree planted by streams of water, which yields its fruit in season and whose leaf does not wither. Whatever he does prospers."

I'm putting this walk alongside my God into perspective this morning. It's a battle of will for me. Stubborn pride is painful. I have had to truly commit in some areas of my own personal daily struggles: to wake up early, to exercise whether rain or shine, eating better, studying His Word more.

And praying. I've always been a believer in the power of prayer. As I woke this morning, my head began talking as soon as my eyes began to open. I heard myself start the doubts and excuses not to move from my bed, and I just started praying humbly to God. As I got dressed, washed up, and did the daily mundane chores of the morning, I continued to talk to Him. He led me to Psalms.

I took complete delight in the Lord this morning, and I meditated on Him and with Him. He guides me throughout the day, but I must seek Him throughout my day. I do this not by griping and groaning when I'm tired and don't want to do the things I've committed to do. I choose to have faith, to believe that He will keep me planted and water me when needed and His fruit will grow. I will not dry up, but grow. It may be a cold winter, but the spring will be so lovely, when I choose to walk in His counsel, and not that of my own or this world.

Remaining a tree planted by streams of water takes work. You must meditate and learn Him to grow in Him, or you will become withered and chaff, as ash to be blown away in the wind. This walk we choose to take in Christ is not for the faint of heart. It's an ongoing commitment; it's conviction daily, and repentance when necessary. It doesn't involve pride or status quo, He wants you to come in humility, humble and willing to hear and heed His instructions.

Let today be a day of spending that time with Him, walking in His counsel hand in hand, step by step. It will be a beautiful and blessed walk for sure.

DAY 3:

TAKE HEED HOW YOU HEAR ...

OCTOBER 5, 2021

One particular verse from Luke, chapter 8, hit me hard in the heart this morning. I read it and pondered over it probably a dozen times or more. As I prayed, I had many other passages come to mind. I actually felt strongly to jot them down. After I did and read upon them, it all made sense. The perfection of His Word was crystal clear.

Luke 8:18, "Therefore consider carefully how you listen. Whoever has will be given more; whoever does not have, even what he thinks he has will be taken from him."

So what is the biggest concern that should fill our minds and hearts, subsequent to just hearing the Word of God?

We should retain the Word of God in our hearts as well as experience its influence appropriately in our personal lives.

But are there means that the Lord has given us, by which He will enable us to both retain the Word in our hearts and experience its influence upon our lives?

Certainly! One of the Lord's means is your own personal supplication. *Pray with all prayer and supplication in the Spirit.* Your personal supplication is one of God's prescribed ways to write the Word of God, which you just heard or read, upon the tablets of your hearts. You must seek the Lord, so that He will inscribe His Word upon the inner sanctuary of your being.

We must also seek for God that He would incline our hearts to *Believe and obey* this particular Word. His Word contains both promises and commands concerning this vital issue. When we turn to the Word, we discover that there are divine commands for us to write the Word of God upon our hearts. However, at the same time, there are also divine promises that it is the work of God to write His Word upon your heart.

Listen to Ezekiel 18:31, concerning what God commands His people to do, "Rid yourselves of all the offenses you have committed, and get a new heart and a new spirit. Why will you die, O house of Israel?" In this verse, we see a command for the rebellious people of ancient Israel to adapt a new heart and a new spirit, for this is the only means to avoid spiritual death and destruction.

And yet, when we turn to Ezekiel 36:26, we discover that it is God who declares that He will accomplish the same reality that He is commanding His people to do.

Ezekiel 36:26, 27, "I will give you a new heart and put a new spirit in you; I will remove from you your heart of stone and give you a heart of flesh. And I will put my spirit in you and move you to follow my decrees and be careful to keep my laws."

So we find a parallel concerning what God commands the people to do and what God promises He will do.

We see this same type of majestic parallel concerning *God's writing His Word upon your heart* in Proverbs 7:1-3, "My son, keep my words, and store up my commands within you. Keep my commands and you will live; guard my teachings as the apple of your eye. Bind them on your fingers; write them on the tablet of your heart."

And yet, at the very same time, this is precisely what God promises that He will do for His people in Jeremiah 31:33, "This is the covenant I will make with the house of Israel after that time, declares the Lord. I will put my law in their minds and write it in their hearts. I will be their God, and they will be my people."

So, is this a hopeless contradiction in terms? No, not at all. This friend is a glorious synthesis of God's amazing revelation. On one hand, God gives this mandate for what the Believer-Christian is (to be and to do), and yet, at the same time, God promises to supply His amazing grace to enable the Believer to live out this reality of faith and obedience. The command from God for, *you to write the Word on your heart* is accompanied with the promise that, ' *your effort, endurance, faith, hard work, and so on … will not be in vain.* For God does not issue a command to a Believer that is not accompanied by His grace to obey it.

If we are going to be a fruitful hearer or reader of His Word, one who retains it so it will be etched in our lives, then we must seek daily the Lord to write the Word upon our hearts. Know that in and of ourselves, we have no power to obey His commands, but God has graciously promised to supply us with His amazing grace when we inquire of Him to work on our behalf.

My prayer this morning is this: Command what you will, Oh Lord; but please Father, grant to me what you command.

DAY 4:

A GENUINE INVESTMENT TO HIM ...

OCTOBER 6, 2021

M atthew 25:31-46, "When the Son of Man comes in his glory, and all the angels with him, he will sit on his throne in heavenly glory. All the nations will be gathered before him, and he will separate the people one from another as a shepherd separates the sheep from the goats. He will put the sheep on his right and the goats on his left. Then the King will say to those on his right, 'Come, you who are blessed by my Father; take your inheritance, the kingdom prepared for you since the creation of the world. For I was hungry and you gave me something to eat, I was thirsty and you gave me something to drink, I was a stranger and you invited me in, I needed clothes and you clothed me, I was sick and you looked after me, I was in prison and you came to visit me.' Then the righteous will answer him, 'Lord, when did we see you hungry and feed you, or thirsty and give you something to drink? When did we see you as a stranger and invite you in, or needing clothes and clothe you? When did we see you sick or in prison and go to visit you?' The King will reply, 'I tell you the truth, whatever you did for one of the least of these brothers of mine, you did for me.' Then he will say to those on his left, 'Depart from me, you who are cursed, into the eternal fire prepared for the devil and his angels. For I was hungry and you gave me nothing to eat, I was thirsty and you gave me nothing to drink, I was a stranger and you did not invite me in, I needed clothes and you did not clothe me, I was sick and in prison and you did not look after me.' They also will answer, 'Lord, when did we see you hungry or thirsty or a stranger or needing clothes or sick or in prison, and did not help you?' He will reply, 'I tell you the truth, whatever you did not do for one of the least of these, you did not do for me.' Then they will go away to eternal punishment, but the righteous to eternal life."

Oh, how this morning's bible reading should prick our hearts deeply, causing us to stop and think about what we invest in daily.

We usually have no problem investing in the passions that drive us in life, those particular gifts and talents we have that come with such ease, but we may find it a little difficult to daily invest in what God has actually called us to do. Sometimes for me it's been my writing and praying. More recently it's been physically moving and getting my body to do what I need it to do without pain and stress. I know God wants my health for me, as I do. I cannot fool myself that my eagerness to do this and gain strength in the physical is about me only. As passionate as I feel toward this journey I've embarked on, I give Him all the glory to do it. For I know full well just how weak I often am to not move as He calls me to do.

You see, our passions often glorify us, where our purpose-filled calling always honors and glorifies God.

Jesus tells us in this passage that when we serve, provide, and sincerely care for the needs of others, we are actually doing these deeds for Him. We often desire that our passion would be our calling, but many times it is not and we must come to understand that passions almost always serve ourselves in some way, and callings assigned to us by God reach out and serve others in ways God desires and that build His kingdom.

Today, as children of God who prepare all our life to enter the kingdom and be placed at His right, let us wisely take the time to daily invest in the calling He has given to us. Let us love our neighbors as ourselves, feeding those who are hungry, giving a drink to those who thirst, clothing one who is naked, giving a kind word to even a stranger, caring for the sick, and visiting the prisoner.

As Christ declares to us in this passage, when we stretch ourselves to do these deeds to invest and provide for others, we are actually doing these deeds of kindness for Him and are investing in His glorious kingdom. May we strive to be faithful and genuine investors.

THE BURDEN OF INCOMPETENCE ...

OCTOBER 7, 2021

2 Corinthians 3:5, "Not that we are competent in ourselves to claim anything for ourselves, but our competence comes from God."

I feel that chapters three through five of 2 Corinthians form one of the Word's great word on ministry, what is involved in representing Christ on this earth.

And not just what has been deemed as our ministry for God—pastoring, teaching, different vocational ministries, and so on—but our personal life deemed ones. Maybe it's our marriage, our parenting, our daily nine to five job.

For me right now it's exercising and eating right. Sometimes it's even in my prayer life.

They're all opportunities to set examples and be Christ-like! And Paul, responding to attacks, defends his ministry. He discusses the ultimate goal of ministry and the grace of God in using "mere jars of clay" to accomplish his work.

Because we're human, at some point we will all experience feelings of inadequacy. Not good enough? Don't measure up?

So, the real issue that you and I face today is not whether we are sufficient for a task God has given us or blessed us to do, but how we respond when a challenge is beyond our capabilities or what we think our capability is at the moment.

You see my friends, oftentimes as an obstacle grows in our mind—let's say the laundry—and we begin to dread having to do it or handle it. We want to run in the opposite direction, away from the challenge and toward safety. We let it go. And it just piles up.

However, avoiding a task that God has given us will lead to only more bondage. We become slaves to that laundry pile.

The more we feed our fears, the more we'll be controlled by those feelings of inadequacy, which can then impact decisions we make and, ultimately, impact our futures. Opportunities are often lost when we let fear overrule our faith.

When God calls you to a task beyond your abilities—maybe you are starting a completely new school; a new job; you have become a new wife, a mother, a grandmother even; whatever it is that has you stuck in these feelings—acknowledge your feelings and then choose to rely on Him and His promises.

By moving forward in faith, despite your fears, you will discover the Lord's faithfulness.

But Paul goes further. The final proof of effectiveness, he says, is people's lives. Your example is the task at hand. The job or the position gives you the opposition.

He always empowers us for the works He assigns, even what we see as mundane chores are established by Him. I know it sounds crazy to think we should feel blessed to clean up our husbands' messes, blessed to take care of crying sick babies all night, blessed to scrub floors and do laundry, but that husband and that home and family that He has blessed you with are in His plan for you. Marriage and motherhood are God-given ministries, too.

Any fears of inadequacy that you can't be a good wife, a good mom, or can't do your job well, it's all lies by the enemy, giving us those anxieties, those oppressive thoughts that leave us frozen in worry and ultimately depressed and feeling defeated.

2 Timothy 1:7, "For God did not give us a spirit of timidity, but a spirit of power, of love and of self-discipline."

Leave those lies at the foot of the cross today. Step into faith and trust His lead as you walk with Him.

DAY 6:
REVERENCE THIS AM ...

OCTOBER 8, 2021

Wow, this speaks volumes! Are we listening?

Job 38:4-11, "Where were you when I laid the earth's foundation? Tell me, if you understand. Who marked off its dimensions? Surely you know! Who stretched a measuring line across it? On what were its footings set, or who laid its cornerstone while the morning stars sang together and all the angels shouted for joy?

Who shut up the sea behind doors when it burst forth from the womb, when I made the clouds its garment and wrapped it in thick darkness, when I fixed limits for it and set its doors and bars in place, when I said, 'This far you may come and no farther; here is where your proud waves halt?'"

When God speaks to Job, He floods the skies with queries, and Job cannot help but get the point. Only God defines God!

You have to know the alphabet before you can read, and God tells Job in His own way, *You don't even know the ABCs of heaven, much less the vocabulary.*

For the first time, Job is quiet. Silenced by a torrent of questions.

The Father's implication is clear, basically saying, *As soon as you are able to handle these simple matters of storing stars and stretching the neck of*

23

the ostrich, then we will have a talk about pain and suffering. But until then, we can do without your commentary.

Wow!

Does Job get the message? I think so. Listen to his response. Job 40:4, "I am unworthy. How can I reply to you? I put my hand over my mouth."

Notice the change? Before he heard God, Job couldn't speak enough. After he heard from God, he couldn't speak at all. Silence was the only proper response.

The word for such moments is a favorite of mine.

One I, too, learned the harder ways of not: reverence.

Stop talking and listen …

Psalms 81:13, "If my people would but listen to me; if Israel would follow my ways … "

When we are hurting, sometimes we find healing by talking about it, maybe with a friend, a loved one, a counselor, to God. But eventually, the time comes to stop talking and listen.

There are times when silence represents the highest respect. The word for such times is reverence.

This was a lesson Job—the man in the Bible most touched by tragedy and despair—learned. If Job had a fault, it was his tongue. He talked too much.

Not that anyone could blame him. Calamity had pounced on him like a lion on a herd of gazelles, and by the time the rampage passed, there was hardly a wall standing or even a loved one living. His own wife told him to, "curse God and die." His four friends came with the bedside manner of drill sergeants, telling him that God is fair, pain is the result of evil, and as sure as two plus two equals four, Job must have some sort of evil in his past to suffer so.

Each had their own interpretation of God and who God is and why God had done what he had done. They weren't the only ones talking about God, though. When his accusers paused, Job himself spent six chapters giving his opinions on God. We are thirty-seven chapters into the book before God clears His throat to speak. And then chapter thirty-eight begins with these words, "Then the Lord answered Job." When the Lord speaks, it's wise to stop talking and just listen.

The Lord was speaking straight to my heart this morning as He reminded me also to stop and listen. How often our reasoning, our ideas, and our assumptions set us up for trips and falls.

We hear to respond and not to understand. We must learn to listen in order to understand so that we may know how He wants us to then respond.

DAY 7:
HE WILL PROVIDE WHEN NEEDED ...

OCTOBER 9, 2021

I nto the book of Ruth this morning. Many people state that the story of Ruth was one of their favorites. For me, I remembered many parts of the story but as I read today I felt that many of us may not be familiar with the whole story. I will try to summarize it for us all.

After God's people in Judah stopped trusting and obeying God, a terrible famine came over the land of Judah. A man named Elimelech with his wife Naomi and their two sons left looking for food. They went to a place called Moab. Once arriving, they learned that the people of Moab worshiped idols.

The sons met and married two Moabite women: Ruth and Orpah. But things for the men in the family did not go so well and Elimelech and his two sons died, leaving Naomi, Ruth, and Orpah.

Naomi, still a believer, heard the Lord had visited and fed his people back in Judah by giving them bread to eat. She decided that with the death of her husband and sons, it was time to return home. Naomi told her two daughters-in-law that because they were Moabites, they could stay in Moab. Naomi actually told them to return to their mothers. Naomi did not want to force them to return with her, but Ruth and Orpah did not want to stay in Moab, they wanted to go with Naomi.

After some discussion, Orpah decided to return to Moab with the people she knew, but Ruth was different. Ruth would not listen to the nonsense coming out of Naomi's mouth and said, "Don't urge me to leave you or to go back from you. Where you go I will go, and where you stay I will stay. Your people will be my people and your God my God." Finally Naomi stopped trying to convince Ruth to leave.

Together they travelled to Bethlehem. Naomi was broken and bitter. She decided that she should not have a positive name like Naomi, which means pleasant, and she would instead be called Mara, which means bitter. Ruth jumped in like she belonged there from the first day they arrived in Bethlehem. Ruth had changed, and was not like the people in Moab. She worshiped the Living God and worked hard in the fields to ensure that both Naomi and her had food to eat. She would actually follow the people harvesting the fields and pick up what was left behind.

The owner of the field was named Boaz, he heard what Ruth was doing and how well she was taking care of her mother-in-law. As a foreigner it was very difficult for Ruth, but Boaz told the harvesters to start leaving grain behind just for Ruth. Ruth told Naomi of this wonderful person named Boaz and Naomi told Ruth that he is a relative. Over time, Boaz wanted to marry Ruth and help take care of Naomi and the family land. But Boaz was not first in line. There was another relative who wanted the land but did not want Ruth, and by law he could not have one without the other. Boaz made a deal with this man and Boaz and Ruth were married. They had a son and named him Obed. Obed was the grandfather of David. Obed was also an ancestor to Jesus.

Now reading and listening to this story, I see that no matter how we are raised and the environment we come from, God is always there waiting for us. We can do wrong, such as worship idols, go off path, and so on, but with the ability to choose, God will help guide us and place people in our lives to help us prosper and grow. At any time Ruth could have gone back to what she knew and how she was raised, but she didn't. She was dedicated to the life Naomi had shown her.

God does not leave us, no matter what the struggle or the trial. We leave him. The choices we make cause us to follow a path that may not be blessed by God, but if we turn back to him, God will open up the path for us to follow.

So, my question for you today is this: Are you a Ruth or are you an Orpah? Either way you choose, you are a child of the one true God and no matter how hard things may be, scraps of food will be there to feed you, just like Ruth. Continue to keep strong and grounded and keep the faith. This life is hard, yes, but without faith and hope in the Lord Jesus Christ, it could be so much harder.

Many times these past few days I wanted to resort back to what I know, the ways and the things I am used to, my comfort zone. God then steps in and reigns me in, reminding me of the One who is providing during this time.

DAY 8:

HIS TRUTH IN HIS PROMISES ...

OCTOBER 10, 2021

The Lord is telling me this morning to not let the distractions around me get me off track. God wants us to be at the ready, prepared to receive the fulfillment of His Word, His truths, and His promises. The Word He has spoken to us and given us are truths of the promises we can expect.

But, we tend to make hearing His Word hard sometimes.

First, we just aren't paying attention. We get easily distracted on our own truths, usually our own expectations and wants. Then we set forth on our own.

Second, we aren't putting in the effort. Are we reading and diving deep into His Word? Are we spending time alone with Him in His truths? Are we walking hand in hand in a relationship with our Lord??

Third, we get lazy. We don't want to get dressed, make the drive, and commune in fellowship at church with other believers gathering to not only hear His Word as we should, but to worship Him and pray for ourselves and others. We make excuses and we defend them too.

Ohhh ... if we were to just do as He tells us to and recognize when we see these steps?

Then we would be holding Him close to our hearts while we wait for His manifestation, answers, and presence! When our fleshly discouragement and doubts come, we need to renew our hearts and our minds in His commitment to our future! He wants our best. He provides His best!

Remember that God is vitally interested in our every success. He is.

But we have to make efforts too.

We can't come to Him in everything if we sit idle in everything He asks of us. Faith takes a little work.

Submission can be tough and painful. Wisdom takes seeking, but then how easily grace and mercy come.

We, too, have to do our part. Being a Christian isn't easy. It's commitment. It's hard. And boy, do distractions come easily! Keep your eyes, ears, and hearts open to Him.

He will never forsake you.

2 Corinthians 7:1, "Since we have these promises, dear friends, let us purify ourselves from everything that contaminates the body and spirit, perfecting holiness out of reverence to God."

DAY 9:
SPIRIT OF BONDAGE ...

OCTOBER 11, 2021

P salms 23:3, "He restores my soul. He guides me in paths of righteousness for his name's sake."

I had the chance to speak briefly last night and this morning with an old friend from Mexico who I had gone on a mission trip to Argentina with many years ago. He asked a question about how do I pray for someone who insists on doing things their way and not God's. When situations arise, they seek fixes of their own reasoning and usually the fast ones instead of seeking God's will for the situations.

He began to tell me that a while ago, he prayed over a woman who had spent several years in prison and gave her life to Christ there. She knew the Word of God very well, and God had changed her life in some ways drastically. Now she was trying to minister to others, but it was not working out well. She was intimidating others with her communication. God told him as he prayed for her one night, *She has an inmate spirit.* He said it was her *Self confidence and security.* She hated insecurity, and could even preach about it for days. In the beginning he said she had called it "authority in Christ," and said that was just the way she was. But her pride blinded her to what was really going on within her.

It's interesting to see that when we rely on our own control of things instead of giving those weak areas to God to use through us and in us for His glory, we fail. Hatred of insecurity is a first sign of an inmate Spirit, a spirit of bondage. Even though this woman was not in prison any more and she is doing well, trying to encourage and minister to others, she is being held back, captive by her insecurities and her abilities to do God's work. It amazes and scares me how the enemy can be so influential once he finds an open door for deception. Then he is on you like white on rice. My friend explained how he asked this woman why she was not able to minister as she was called to do. Soon, the Holy Spirit broke her will, and showed her that without meekness in Christ, there is no power.

The truth is the opposite of what the world believes. The more you humble yourself, the more God elevates you. Her tough-guy persona was her way of surviving in life, but she was held bondage by that attitude and way of thinking, like a ball and chain. It was a chain she needed to let go of, and allow God to be there for her instead, leading her where to go, showing her what to do and exactly when to do it.

Once the truth was actually revealed, this woman was set free and didn't have to look or act so tough and confident anymore. She could cry when she needed to and wail out for help on her knees when she was broken inside. All those other masks, those shows, were part of that chain in her life. Now she can enjoy life and friendships without the masks.

Many of us have rough pasts that hold us as captive in one aspect or another, a bad habit that is hard to stop. My diet and exercise are an example. So is wanting to jump in and fix our kids' issues every time they make a poor decision or a mistake. I also struggle with wanting to see my family happy and healthy, making good decisions and living for the Lord. When one messes up and the consequences come and come down hard, I suffer too, sometimes more than they do. Why? Because I love them. Because I hate to see them hurt or to struggle.

I've had to submit that control to the Lord many times. Even after I sought my own fixes and my own answers first, He had to sometimes break me for me to turn to Him in my need.

A lesson of right and wrong? No. A lesson of endurance, patience, and pushing aside pride and saying, "Yes, I did wrong." Admittance and acceptance of my actions, of trying to do and say and handle life on my own, without my Father's help or guidance, that's a lesson in itself. I, too, struggle with the urge to want to fix everybody else's problems. I can't, but my God can. And the best thing I can do to help, without wearing myself thin and making myself stressed or sick or unhappy in my work, is simple: Pray. Pray for them. Pray for ears to hear God's Words of guidance. Pray for eyes to see God's Word before them to lead them. And pray for hearts to open and be filled with His spirit to live as they should be living.

Remember, you don't have to be in prison to have a prison-like spirit over you. There are many addictions to choose from, and the enemy will use them all. Food, alcohol, drugs, medications, we can even be addicted to being sick, seeking doctors and medications to heal us. Pornography, self reliance and control, pride and ego, smoking, diet, and exercise. We tend to overdo it. So, examine yourself and your heart daily. And if you need to be set free of bondage, pray for it! Because living that way is no way to live and will accomplish nothing for God and His glory. It will only cause more hurdles for you in your walk with Him.

DAY 10:
HE HOLDS ON TO ME ...

OCTOBER 12, 2021

Isaiah 41:13, "For I am the Lord, your God, who takes hold of your right hand and says to you, Do not fear; I will help you."

I was hurting and sore this morning, tired of getting up earlier than normal.

The weather was dark and it was dreary. I had every excuse in the book not to get up.

I saw a big bright sun in the sky this morning. As I walked hard and used those arm weights through it, I watched as the sun shined, even behind the clouds! Shining through the darkness. Shining through the dreary wet damp morning, there it was. I still could see the light in my doubts and excuses this morning!

That's what Jesus does for me. He is with me in everything. He is walking beside me. He is. And for that I am forever grateful.

He holds on to me. He does. Through it all. Every time I argue His way and stray off, He takes my hand, yet again, and guides me right back to His side.

This song, in my heart, was my morning motivation. It reminded me of many blessings, too: The specific woman who graciously took time to send it to me this morning; the many women who have been praying and encouraging me to get up and go every day; the many other friends and family who are praying and supporting me throughout this journey, and just how blessed I am to have each and every one of them in my life. He has blessed me in this walk. He truly has already. I know that the best is yet to come. And He is holding me through it all, so delicately and yet so firmly.

Isaiah chapters 40 through 46 echo the sweet chapters at the end of the book of Job. The Lord shows Himself as master of the universe. Before Him, nations are like a drop in a bucket (40:15) and people are like grasshoppers (40:22). He taunts all other so-called gods; such idols are carved of the same tree used to cook supper (44:12-20). The true God, the God of the Israelites, is the one who created the universe (45:12,18), who called Abraham (41:8), and who rescued the Jews from slavery in Egypt. For the dispirited Jewish survivors of Babylon's invasion, this exalted view of God was a reminder, just as it is for me this morning! It is a reminder that God has neither vanished nor rejected them.

My mind and my heart are reminded of a song, *Hold on to Me*. It speaks about His grasp on you throughout every struggle: when barely breathing, when feeling unworthy, when in the dark, and when we have turned away, He is still holding on to us. How uplifting and encouraging to know my God is ready to hold me in everything I come to, the good things and the not so good things, the easy times and the really hard times. To have that peace and the reassurance that, even when I lose my grip, He is still there to rest in, because there is no one who loves me more.

Oh what a beautiful freedom that gives! When I forget, my God reminds me.

DAY 11:
ARE YOU BELIEVING FOR IT ...

OCTOBER 13, 2021

J ames 1:12, "Blessed is the man who perseveres under trial, because when he has stood the test, he will receive the crown of life that God has promised to those who love Him."

And yet again this morning I found myself neck deep in unbelief, wrestling with my own knowledge of getting up and moving. As I walked this morning, that sun was rising yet again, and it felt like He did that just for me!

I am reminded by the shine of the sun that He can move the unmovable. I have to trust Him for it and through it. When we let those false beliefs come into our minds and designate our hearts, we lose. The battle in our minds, our bodies, our physical flesh belongs to God. And when we take it upon our own doings and our own determination to conquer our goals, we may see the end results to completion. But where was the growth of the fruits in it? What brought on that self-righteous fruition? I want my God's hand in this with me, because I know it will not be in vain, my victory in Him. It will not go to waste. It won't be temporary. It will only grow and prosper in Him.

Allowing His strength for me and His ways in me through this daily walk will bring on growth in everything inside me. My physical, my mental, and my spiritual life will only flourish.

Is it hard? Yes, it is. But God never said walking with Him would be easy. He said take up your cross and walk with me. Today He is leading me in doing just that, walking with me, right at my side. And I'm so grateful for His mercy and His gracious love while setting the pace for me.

I pray you go as He leads you today, confident as He walks beside you through whatever your day brings.

DAY 12:

HE IS AS FAITHFUL
AS THE SUNRISE ...

OCTOBER 14, 2021

I n my battles this day, I battle my weakness, my strong will of control yet
again. And He grants me grace, which turns my control back to Him.
His mercy this morning restores my hope. He is so worthy of my song this
morning. There are blessings for obedience, as well as curses for disobedience.
He has led me straight to Deuteronomy 28.

In the first fourteen verses, Moses is speaking to the Israelites. He
tells them to fully obey the Lord and states the blessings that will follow as
they do so. Blessings will come upon them and accompany them when they
listen and obey Him (verse 2). He will establish them as a holy people as He
promised them by oath, if they keep the commands of the Lord their God
and walk in His ways (verse 9).

In all His goodness, there are still consequences when we turn our back
to Him and His commands. Deuteronomy 28:16-68 states all of this. There
are repercussions for our disobedience as well.

Moses states there will be confusion and He will rebuke everything
they put their hand to. He will allow diseases to enter the land and they will
suffer them. There will be heat and drought. The rains will be dust and ash.

I pray as you take time to read this chapter today that God touches your heart and gently nudges you to realize those things that you may need to give to Him to handle, and relinquish that control too; that obedience to Him will enter your heart so fully that you will see His sunshine; that His mercy rains down and restores your hope this morning or afternoon or night as you hear Him speak to you. Old habits do die hard. Leave them at His feet, and ask Him to move for you when you just feel you can't.

This day of devotion, let's together be obedient and walk in His ways just as Moses instructed in verse 9.

Let us not grow weary in obedience to Him during this walk. Remember that we are not alone and He is our comfort, our hope, and our victory. Allow His spirit to dwell, deeply rooted inside us, as we continue walking in His ways.

DAY 13:
AN ATTITUDE OF PRAYER ...

OCTOBER 15, 2021

T oday as I started my morning routine I obsessed about and tried to intricately schedule my prayer time, workout time, Bible study time, and writing time.

I'm reminded of Matthew 6:5-8, "And when you pray, do not be like the hypocrites, for they love to pray standing in the synagogues and on the street corners to be seen by men. I tell you the truth, they have received their reward in full. But when you pray, go into your room, close the door and pray to your Father, who is unseen. Then your Father, who sees what is done in secret, will reward you. And when you pray do not keep on babbling like pagans, for they think they will be heard because of their many words. Do not be like them, for your Father knows what you need before you ask Him."

It spoke to my heart, and I recognized that I prayed while getting out of the bed this morning and as I went about making my morning coffee. While taking the dogs out, feeding them, and then driving to my workout, I was listening, singing, and worshipping God in the car. We spoke Godly conversations during our workout. I prayed and worshipped Him on my ride home. I even got to share Jesus with a lady at the store. All before 9:30 a.m. Alleluia and Amen, my heart sings to that!

Now, I do agree that we all should schedule time with our Lord everyday, in quiet and in complete focus on Him. During my stress of schedules these past days, I lost the realization that I commune with Him all day long, and that I should be. We all should be!! My drives in the car anywhere should be shared with Him. My workouts should be alongside Him. The store visits, too. I should be bringing Him and speaking to Him and having an ongoing relationship with Him all throughout my day. It should be no different than speaking and doing things with my husband and my family. I should be constantly in communication with Him, where it shows in my entire day. The folks I am scheduled to be with as well as those I meet throughout my day.

How awesome is that? All day we are sharing stories. He knows my life., the good, the bad, and the ugly! And even though He knows the outcomes of it all, He doesn't get bored of my prayers and our one-on-one time together. He wants me to talk to Him about my life. He wants to hold me up through it. He wants to encourage me in it. And when I am not in His presence, walking beside Him, He graciously nudges me and pulls me back into that commune with Him.

It's a blessing to have other believers so deeply and richly living in His Spirit that they will willingly call you, text you, or stop and pray for you when God speaks to them to do so.

We all cringe at the word, accountability. I'm basking in the blessing of that today.

And as believers, sisters and brothers in Christ and of Christ, we should want to be that encouragement to others in their needs and pray for them, too. He is a good, good, Father.

And He blesses us in so many ways in our obedience.

DAY 14:
AWAKE MY SOUL ...

P salm 55:16-19, "But I call to God, and the Lord saves me. Evening, morning, and noon I cry out in distress, and He hears my voice. He ransoms me unharmed from the battle waged against me, even though many oppose me. God who is enthroned forever, will hear them and afflict them-men who never change their ways and have no fear of God."

The Lord our God is working as I lay my petitions and supplications before Him this day. As I come to His throne in reverence this morning, I feel His presence so strongly. I feel a restoration of comfort and hope for today's walk.

Waking was tough this morning. The excuses came like a flood. My muscles cried in pain and my joints fought me with stiffness. As I came to Him in prayer and kept myself in His Word before the start of my day, things shifted. When I have His truths laid out before me in black and white, His blessed assurance to guide me. When He blesses me to even just hear my pleas in my distresses, whether it be aches and pains of the physical or of the heart. I leave His presence knowing He and I together will follow through. His promises to me and my submissions to Him.

He keeps my heart steadfast. He makes me continue to walk in His ways and in His guidance. It's His strength that empowers me in the ache. His hope encourages me not to quit.

Spending this special quiet time with Him daily in the early part of the day fills me and restores my hopes and my fire for Him throughout the rest of my day.

Psalm 57:7-8, "My heart is steadfast, O God, my heart is steadfast; I will sing and make music. Awake, my soul! Awake, harp and lyre! I will awaken the dawn."

DAY 15:

UNEXPECTED OBSTACLES ...

OCTOBER 17, 2021

D aniel 6:34, "Now Daniel so distinguished himself among the administrators and the satraps by his exceptional qualities that the king planned to set him over the whole kingdom. At this the administrators and satraps tried to find grounds for charges against Daniel in his conduct of government affairs, but they were unable to do so. They could find no corruption in him, because he was trustworthy and neither corrupt nor negligent."

There are days where I have made my own plans to conquer and accomplish, but as my day plays out those plans go out the window. Something goes off my schedule, and the day changes from what I had planned. Sometimes my attitude in those moments changes too.

I begin to get discouraged, and I lose my stamina. I have even found myself griping about it. It is in those times, those moments of despair, where I am reminded and even urged by the Lord to be still and just pray.

Daniel was made a big deal! He became a prime minister to Babylon. And then he is told he cannot pray to his God, only to the King. And what does he do? He takes those feelings—probably of discontent, worry, confusion, and fear—straight to the Father.

Daniel, 6: 10-11, "Now when Daniel learned that the decree had been published, he went home to his upstairs room where the windows opened toward Jerusalem. Three times a day he got down on his knees and prayed, giving thanks to his God, just as he had done before. Then these men went as a group and found Daniel praying and asking God for help."

We can be respectful and diligent when dealing with daily issues that arise and never compromise our faith, just as Daniel was while working for pagan kings. The book of Daniel offers us a wonderful model of how to live with unexpected obstacles and still serve others who do not share or even respect our beliefs.

During this day I pray to be prompted to be in faith and prayer when unexpected obstacles arise, such as pains, worries, even defiance in my own flesh! When I go straight to Him with my requests and my needs, He is faithful to answer. He guides me and He even protects me when it is needed.

DAY 16:
MY PROTECTION ...

OCTOBER 18, 2021

P salm 3:1-4, "O Lord, how many are my foes! How many rose up against me! Many are saying of me, 'God will not deliver him.' But you are a shield around me, O Lord; you bestow glory on me and lift up my head. To the Lord I cry aloud, and He answers me from His holy hill."

This past weekend was difficult for me in the diet department for sure. I was eating out and not being as structured in my portion control as I have been all week, and it threw me off track. Eating snacks later than I should have been wasn't any help either. Yes, indeed it has been a challenge for me. Food has truly been a comfort and a habit to me in the evenings. I have had no problems with eating in my bed at 9 or 10 p.m. in the past.

This morning when I saw there wasn't a significant weight loss this week except half of a pound, defeat and despair set into my heart like a flaming spear was shot directly at me. Every doubt began to creep in along with every excuse and thought to just give up, give in, and throw up the white flag in defeat on this diet and exercise thing I had started.

Just as those thoughts entered into my mind, my heart felt heavy with conviction. I could hear God saying to me, *This thing you started? I recall walking with you, hand in hand, my dear. And I do not quit! I will bring you to a place of wholeness and goodness and victory in your obedience to me. And I will protect you from defeat.*

As I heard those words in my mind, my heart went to Romans 8:28-37. He reminded me of being called by His purpose. That I was predestined to be conformed to the likeness of His Son! And that this will all be glorified in praise to Him!

If God is for me, who can be against me? As I prayed and spent time in His presence this morning, He led me to Psalms, reminding me that He is a shield around me. He bestows glory on me and lifts up my head. When I choose to cry out to Him in my weakness.

Psalm 5:11-12, "But let all that take refuge in you be glad: let them ever sing for joy. Spread your protection over them, that those who love your name may rejoice in you. For surely, O Lord, you bless the righteous; you surround them with your favor as with a shield."

Today I pray in refuge to my Lord. I sing His joy and His praises.

Knowing He is protecting me from the enemy's attacks on my mind and my heart. My doubts and insecurities are left yet again at my Lord's feet, believing His favor is with me and His shield covers me as we walk together throughout this journey.

When the enemy attacks you in your weakness, take it straight to the source of true strength. The Protector, The Lord that will hold you up and sustain you through them. He will lead you in truth and guide you in His strength. He wants to lead you to victory in Him today and every day.

DAY 17:

CONTENT IN HIM ...

OCTOBER 19, 2021

P salm 131, "My heart is not proud, O Lord, my eyes are not haughty; I do not concern myself with great matters or things too wonderful for me. But I have stilled and quieted my soul; like a weaned child with its mother, like a weaned child in my soul within me. O Israel, put your hope in the Lord both now and forevermore."

As I spent time with the Lord in prayer this morning, God had me read through this verse over and over again. Having structure and schedules aren't always easy or fun. But I tell you that doing this and committing myself to commune with Him on a true one-on-one level has been such a joy and a blessing. This verse spoke so profoundly to my heart. Let me share this with you today. Let this encourage and uplift your spirit.

How trusting is a baby? Not very, some would say, for babies tend to cry, sometimes violently, as soon as they feel the slightest hunger. The lost scent of momma when in the arms of another sends them in a tizzy. But it is the weaned child, a little older, who has learned to trust its mother, to fret less and simply ask for food or comfort instead of wailing and having a tantrum. The profound simplicity of this patience is David's model for how he, and all of Israel, should wait on the Lord. The apostle Paul comments similarly in Philippians 4:12-13, "I know what it is to be in need, and I know what it is to have plenty. I have learned the secret of being content in any and every situation, whether well fed or hungry, whether living in plenty or in want. I can do everything through him who gives me strength!"

My prayer today is that you too have such contentment in your heart and your spirit, knowing He is all that you need! He will provide and keep you in and through all things. May we never get brazen and prideful in our hearts during our trials and struggles when turning to the Lord is no longer our want but a last-ditch effort. I don't want to allow myself to ever get so persistent in my own ways that when all else fails I am left alone, crying out to Him, but instead as soon as difficulty arises and is recognized just to simply ask of Him in everything, in every circumstance, believing and knowing that my hope is in Him always and trusting in His guidance.

DAY 18:

A CALL AND A PROMISE ...

OCTOBER 20, 2021

H aggai 1:5, "Now this is what the Lord God Almighty says: 'Give careful thought to your ways. You have planted much but harvested little. You eat but never have enough. You drink but never have your fill. You put on clothes, but are not warm. You earn wages, only to put them in a purse with holes in it.'"

In Haggai this morning, I read how sometimes, at crucial moments, a single voice can stir a directionless mass of people to action. Haggai's words rang clear in a time of confusion. The Jews came back from their exile in Babylon, but seemed to have forgotten the point of returning. After a false start on the temple, they devoted their energy to building their own houses, and the ruins of Solomon's temple stood as a nagging reminder that they neglected God.

Haggai urged them to "give careful thought" to their situation. He didn't rage like Jeremiah or build poems like Isaiah. He put it simply and logically: You worked hard, but what for? Crops didn't grow. Money disappeared as soon as it was earned. Why?

Because they had mistaken their priority. They didn't put God first (verse 7). "This is what the Lord God Almighty says: 'Give careful thought to your ways.' Go up into the mountains and bring down timber and build the house, so that I may take pleasure in it and be honored, says the Lord."

And just like the people responded to Haggai, I heard Him this morning telling me the same message. "Jennifer, I am with you!"

Haggai 2:4-5 states, "'But now be strong, O Zerubbabel,' declares the Lord. 'Be strong, O Joshua son of Jehozadak, the high priest. Be strong, all you people of the land,' declares the Lord,' and work. For I am with you,' declares the Lord God Almighty. 'This is what I covenanted with you when you came out of Egypt. And my Spirit remains among you. Do not fear.'"

There have been times when I hear His voice so clearly and I follow it in hot pursuit, only to then find that I drift off to my own ideas and my own ways, leaving God's words to me and His ways for me to the sidelines. I run ahead of Him and I make my own plans and even execute them, all in vain.

We must always give careful thought to God's words, listening and obeying. And when confusion happens, continue doing what He has told you already and then pray and seek Him in it until He tells you differently, knowing that He will bless you for it and be with you through it.

DAY 19:
WALKING WITH GOD ...

OCTOBER 21, 2021

P roverbs 3:5-6, "Trust in the Lord with all your heart and lean not on your own understanding; in all your ways acknowledge him, and he will make your paths straight."

God was truly speaking to my heart this morning as I prayed for the day ahead. The list of prayer requests this morning seemed to be endless. My heart felt heavy. I was outside at 6:30 a.m. I could hear thunder in the distance as I was praying. I opened my Bible to Proverbs 3 and I just began to read each word carefully. Chapter 3 speaks of some benefits of wisdom. I encourage you to take the time to read this full chapter and truly bask in the words written.

As I finished and prayed to God asking Him to open my heart and my mind to His Word, verses 5-6 stuck in my head. "In all your ways acknowledge Him." It is so literal. It spoke to my heart saying, *In all your ways Jennifer, know Me. Know your God!*

This fundamental statement of how to relate to my Father implies more than just mere reverence. You see, my friends, nodding in God's direction today or tomorrow simply is not enough: we must truly acknowledge Him by living closely with Him and relating to Him personally in every single aspect of our lives.

Following and obeying are hand in hand when walking with the Lord. Conversations with Him are to be as easy and as necessary as communication with a spouse or loved one. He wants us to know Him on a deep, personal level. We must have a solid relationship that is continuously growing, as we spend more time with Him, learn more of Him, and grow deeper into love with our Savior and Lord.

Trusting as He leads and confident that when we stumble, His hand will be there to hang on to and gain our balance and sure footing to continue our walk together. Having such faith and confidence in God blesses my heart this morning. It encourages me and builds me up for the day ahead, to recognize my blessings and acknowledge Him in my walk always.

DAY 20:

REMEMBERING BACK ...

OCTOBER 22, 2021

Psalm 77:11-15, "I will remember the deeds of the Lord; yes I will remember your miracles of long ago. I will meditate on all your works and consider all your mighty deeds. Your ways, O God, are holy. What god is so great as our God? You are the God who performs miracles; you display your power among the peoples. With your mighty arm you redeemed your people, the descendants of Jacob and Joseph."

Some mornings I have the alarm set and He wakes me an hour or more before it sounds. Someone or something immediately comes to my mind. Sometimes it's a prompt for me to pray, either for myself or for another. Sometimes it's anxieties and worries about the day's start. Then tomorrow's plans creep in. And by the time I get out of the bed to begin to seek His Wor and pray, I'm already thinking of next week. I'm sure many of you understa these mornings.

Today, reading Psalm 77 takes me back to beautiful past circum when the Lord showed up and showed out in my distress. And wha by beautiful, others may consider as tragedy, or trauma even. But m serves as His beacon of Hope, remembering back to all He has and all the prayers He has answered in my life!

"I will remember the deeds of the Lord; yes I will remember your miracles of long ago." That verse has such profound meaning and brings prayers of gratitude and praise to my heart.

Psalm 77 is a remembering poem. It starts with deep despair. From verses 1-9, will He reject me forever? Will He ever show favor again? Has He forgotten to be merciful? Has He in anger withheld His compassion?

Then thoughts turn, deliberately, to the past. Remember the turmoil at the banks of the Red Sea? Could anything be worse? But in that moment, they saw the Lord's power: He led them to safety in an impossible crisis. He would do the same again!

This morning I prayed in thanksgiving, counting numerous blessings and some undeserved favors. And through remembering in prayer, I am strengthened by Him to face the future and to recommit myself to trust His care and provisions. It is such an amazing blessing to be able to pray and have Him remind us of how He has handled those impossibilities of the past, because His hope shines ever so much brighter to us then. He keeps His promise to love us!

Let today be a day of gratitude to Him, remembering His promises ˋ and just. His will for us is perfect. When we are feeling rebellious, ˀ or forgetful, be reminded of His power!

ˡed of earlier failings, to strive for victorious outcomes. ˙stent and wonderful He has been through it all.

when laying awake, and turn your thoughts to what He has done, and He will do it again.

DAY 21:

INSTRUCTIONS TO OVERCOME ...

OCTOBER 23, 2021

1 Timothy 4:7-10, "Have nothing to do with godless myths and old wives' tales; rather, train yourself to be godly. For physical training is of some value, but godliness has value for all things, holding promise for both the present life and the life to come. This is a trustworthy saying that deserves full acceptance (and for this we labor and strive), that we have put our hope in the living God, who is the Savior of all men, and especially of those who believe."

As I read this morning in 1 Timothy, I felt the Lord pulling at my heartstrings during these verses as I read them over to myself. I noticed how Paul used the analogy of physical training in his letter to Timothy, urgin him to train himself in godliness the same way disciplined athletes t for competition.

I too have had to overcome many physical barriers in my life. T faced personality barriers. Several times Paul refers to Timothy's timid disposition, which probably contributed to his chronically ach. Given his shyness and half Jew, half Gentile ancestry, Tim seem the ideal choice for a heresy fighter in a turbulent church was convinced he was the man for the job. He reminded ordination, a commitment he had made long before. He encouraged him with motivational phrases, "I charge you," and "I urge you."

Sometimes as Christians we feel harassed, almost. Yes, at times from others, and sometimes from ourselves. We need a model, an example of how we should live, perhaps even more than that. We need words of wisdom. In 1 Timothy, Paul urges his loyal friend to become that model by accepting the discipline and hard work required of him.

These past twenty-one days have been a rollercoaster for me, in discipline, hard work, schedules, prayer, and writing. My self tends to want to do things the easier way. My head talks of doubts and fears. My heart grows heavy under that weight. My ego rises.

We all have traits, habits, and issues we carry with us, and barriers that hinder our growth and walk in faith with Him. But He urges us to persevere and overcome them. Just as Paul did for Timothy, I urge each of you to consider what has been that barrier between you and God today. I pray that you acknowledge it and submit it to your Father, then train in His words and His ˑv. Our calling is to be godly in whatever we say or do. By training and preˑ for the challenge, we are equipped with all our needs to be victorious.

ˑtimes it's hard work, harder than we expected or ever experiˑ ˑr our good, to mold us and create us, to do what He wants ˑway. I encourage you to read 1 Timothy, to read how he ˑhe Lord by persevering and with his friend Paul's ˑnt. Let's be that for each other. It's such a blessˑ ˑo and have help from others. It's time to get ˑainst all odds my friends, we overcome

LEARN TO FOLLOW INSTRUCTION ...

OCTOBER 23, 2021

J oshua 1:6-9, "Be strong and courageous, because you will lead these people to inherit the land I swore to their forefathers to give them. Be strong and very courageous. Be careful to obey all the law my servant Moses gave you; do not turn from it to the right or to the left, that you may be successful wherever you go. Do not let this Book of the Law depart from your mouth; meditate on it day and night, so that you may be careful to do everything written in it. Then you will be prosperous and successful. Have I not commanded you? Be strong and courageous. Do not be terrified; do not be discouraged, for the Lord your God will be with you wherever you go."

Learning to follow instructions is so important to walking in a relationship with God. God showed us that yesterday. And this morning as I prayed about it, He led me straight to Joshua, yet again granting me access (instruction) to exactly how to go about that.

Once inside Canaan, the Israelites followed God's instructions precisely, even when doing so must have strained their faith to new limits. The people of Jericho had shut themselves behind stone walls, waiting for the onslaught of the feared Israelites. But how did the Israelites spend their first week in Canaan? They built a stone monument to God, performed circumcision rituals, and held a Passover celebration. No conquering army had ever behaved in such a manner.

Everything in Joshua feels handpicked this morning to strike home the point that God was really in charge. Covering a period of several years, out of twenty-four chapters there are only a few sentences referring to some extensive military campaigns (ch.10-11). But key events, like the fall of Jericho, got detailed coverage, underscoring that the Israelites succeeded when they relied on God, not military might. The few negative stories (the battle of Ai and the trick of the Gibeonites) show what happened when the Israelites did not seek God's will.

What then should we take away from this?

The Bible does not give history for its own sake. Rather, it presents practical and spiritual lessons. Thankfully, Joshua's lessons are overwhelmingly positive ones. The Israelites had positive results when they were guided by God. In fact, the book concludes that, "Not one of all the Lord's good promises to the house of Israel failed; every one was fulfilled" (21:45).

Today, whatever is on your plate, let this be a fresh breeze of hope. Following God works, Joshua shows us that. We can't allow our circumstances to deter us left or right from what God tells us is straight ahead. He will be with us through the work, through the struggle, to the end result. And it will be glorious, because it was in Him the victory. Follow His lead. You have access to every instruction. Don't just read them, live them.

DAY 23:

RISE OR ROT ...

OCTOBER 25, 2021

M ark 4:9, "Then Jesus said, 'He who has ears to hear, let him hear.'" Many times throughout our days, we hear God's Word spoken to us. At the church we attend. In music we may listen to. From folks that we engage in Godly conversation with. Things are spoken to us and from us. Those things spoken of Christ are like seeds. Some are graciously accepted, while others are kicked to the dust. But when we share Christ with others or He is shared with us, those seeds of love, joy, peace, and forgiveness have the power to grow.

There have been conversations and messages presented to me in my life that I did not receive. I could not receive them at that time. I was tangled in a web of sin, like chains. My ears were open and I heard the words, but my heart wasn't accepting. The seeds bounced off and never took root.

Mark 4:11-12, "He told them, 'The secret of the kingdom of God has been given to you. But to those on the outside everything is said in parables so that, they may be ever seeing but never perceiving, and ever hearing but never understanding; otherwise they might turn and be forgiven!'"

Jesus spoke in these parables so our minds could understand His Father's ways, because the Lord's ways are not our ways. We can't fathom His understanding. It is too much for our minds to comprehend. I encourage you to read Mark chapter 4:1-20. It is the parable of the sower.

When a seed has been sown to us like His Word, what happens to that seed? Are we easily allowing the enemy to scoop it up? Or are we full of joy when hearing the Word on Sunday, then go home to never hear or speak it again until next Sunday? Are we distracted from tending to the seed with life's worries, desires, and stresses?

What if we allowed that seed to take root? What if we tended to it daily? In prayer, attending church regularly, and joining a Bible class or studies? What about praise and worshipping daily, not just Sunday in the church house? What about at home, in the shower; as you clean and do housework; on your daily commute; your workouts even?

We have opportunities all day to accept seeds sown our way and to sow seeds to others. Whether fruit is grown or not, seeds are still important. Seeds are necessary for growth. Hearing His Word is vital to sowing seeds. They need that nurturing. They need the Son. They need water and nourishment of the type that only He can provide. But they also need darkness for a while. Being planted and rooting firmly can be harder than you think. A seed is under ground, under pressure and weight. Alone sometimes, in the dark. But all that time if it is fed, nourished, and watered, and has the light of the sun shining on it regularly, it will grow into fruit. The (son) won't leave its place above that seed, shining on it as it grows.

Today, let's be reminded of those seeds we plant and the seeds that have been planted in us along our walk. Recognize them and tend to them daily. Let's pray against the temptations of the enemy to steal them from us. Nor will they be thorns to us, only to be choked to unfruitfulness. Tend to your seeds, my friends. Fill yourself with God everyday, in every way possible, and produce such a growth that His fruits are plentiful in you. Share them. Spread those seeds every way you can in conversations, a phone call, a text, the waiter at the diner, the bill collector calling, when volunteering within your community, by sharing your testimony in Christ to others, or simply by sharing your walk and your experiences of God on paper. Let's not forget to tend to them.

DAY 24:
A TIME FOR ...

OCTOBER 26, 2021

I studied Ecclesiastes 3 this morning as my body speaks to me about aches and pains. My eyes cry out to me, heavy with sleep. My knees shake under the weight of the walk to come. The Lord in my prayers reminds me that there is indeed a time for everything, a season for every activity under heaven (verse 1).

As you read this chapter, the teacher explains that all the time in life that God gives us has purpose. Time to live and time to die. Time to plant and time to sow. Time to kill and time to heal. Time to be silent and time to speak. Time to love and time to hate. From verses two through eight, he lists them.

Yet in verse 9, he asks, What does a worker gain from his toil?

He reminds us how even when at work for the Lord, there is time to get the job done in His will and way and time, and also a time to enjoy the work and rest even during it all, knowing that everything He does will endure forever. Nothing can be added to it or taken from it. God does it so men will revere Him.

As you continue with verses 15-21, the talk goes to a man's fate. It's the same as the animals. They live as the other lives, and one does as the other does. They all have the same breath. Man has no advantage over the animal.

All go to the same place and come from the same dust, only to return to that dust.

What filled me this morning was realizing that all this is for His purpose. This is now His time to grow and mold and shape me. I want nothing more than to enjoy this time and this work He is doing in me, because this is my lot. And bringing this to fruition is His want and my prayer, that after it is done, it remains. Here for another to see, to hear, and to learn, and to know His work. What He is. Who He is. And what He has done and will continue to do.

If you hear His call to you, then heed it and follow. This time is for you and Him. It was planned. It has a purpose. And it is just for you. Find joy in it. Peace in it. Song in it! I'm reminded of a Disney cartoon, *Snow White*, I believe it is. As she worked hard to clean that messy dwarves cottage and was overwhelmed by her work at hand, she knew to "whistle while you work." And so the song went and joy grew and she cleaned and toiled till the cottage was clean and shining.

What if we turned our attitudes to sing as we worked for Him?

How much sweeter would that work be? *Use this time wisely*, I hear God telling me. *Soak in it, Jennifer. Speak about it. Share it. And I will bless it and use it for a time after yours has come and gone.*

That blesses and fills my heart to know. I pray this encourages you, my friends, in whatever time you find yourself in today. Use it wisely. Walk with Him during it. Enjoy the toiling. He will use all of it for good! And it will endure for time beyond our own.

Ecclesiastes 3:22, "So I saw that there is nothing better for a man than to enjoy his work, because that is his lot. For who can bring him to see what will happen after him."

DAY 25:
A REBELLIOUS HEART ...

OCTOBER 27, 2021

I saiah 1 is what my heart soaked in this morning. Isaiah 1:2, "Hear O heavens! Listen, O earth! For the Lord has spoken: 'I reared children and brought them up, but they have rebelled against me.'"

Too much religion, not enough obedience. Isaiah paints a striking picture of the conditions in Judah at this time. Luxury indicates the nation was prospering economically well. There was no shortage of offerings, prayers, and religious celebrations (verses 11-17).

But Isaiah condemned Judah for not putting religion into practice by defending the weak people, such as the widows and the fatherless. The country's prosperity had come at the poor's expense.

Some days my offerings and my prayers feel unworthy. They feel begged instead of blessed. They become repetitive and daunting even. This reminded me that He doesn't need my offerings, my work, or my toil. It's my heart He longs after. Too much is sometimes no good.

Why do we run ahead of our Father so often? We hear Him, but we don't truly take the time to listen to Him. This chastisement used to hurt me.

It brought me quickly to anger, to doubt, to disgust and despair. This morning, it brings me to a sweet place, though, as I read verse 18.

"'Come now, let us reason together,' says the Lord. 'Though your sins are like scarlet, they shall be white as snow; though they are red as crimson, they shall be like wool. If you are obedient, you will eat the best from the land; but if you resist and rebel, you will be devoured by the sword.' For the mouth of the Lord has spoken."

He wants to reason together. How absolutely wonderful is it that the Lord God wants to take the time and the love to reason to me? I am but a wretch, and He still cares for me and values me to take His gentle mercy and reason with me in His grace! Oh, when I think of His love for us.

You see, my friends, Isaiah was like the Shakespeare of Hebrew literature. The New Testament quotes him more than all of the other prophets combined. And yet as he lived at such a crucial time, war was waged all around him. As he began his work, the people seemed strong and wealthy. But the signs of danger were rampant. Folks were using their power to oppress the poor. Men went around drunk; women cared more about their clothes than their neighbor's hunger. People gave lip service to God and kept the appearance of religion up, but did little more. Isaiah didn't temper his message for the sake of the popular vote. His words were harsh about what needed to change.

How often has a good deed gone to a public performance? Do we walk by the hungry to indulge our own hunger with those we only see fit to eat with? How easy it is to forget what our true jobs are and what our true purpose is when the blessings flow abundantly. Sadly, we don't honor Him and use those blessings to bless others as we should. When the food is plentiful, who are we feeding? We don't have a pecking order, at least we shouldn't! We need to feed all who are hungry. I know I've gotten forgetful in my past deeds and lost sight of what and even where God wanted me to be, only seeing my part, my work, my perspective of the task at hand. Then only to gain in prosperity and forget how and who gave it to me.

These daily reminders from our Father are rich in nourishment to our spirit if we take them in. These, my friends, are words to savor this morning. Be careful in our calling to not lose sight of Him and His ways. Obey His words and follow His lead. Never look down at your feet as you walk with Him, look up to the One in control of the walk. Oh, how we forget when things are good.

DAY 26:

REST IN HIM ...

OCTOBER 28, 2021

I am deep in the mindset of rest this morning, something I find hard to do. Rest is defined as peace, ease, or refreshment. To relax is to become loose or less firm; to have a mild manner, or to be less stiff.

The bible speaks highly of rest. It is a repeated theme throughout scripture, beginning in Genesis 2:2-3, where God created for six days and then He rested, setting the standard for mankind to follow.

The ten commandments made rest a requirement of the law (Exodus 20:8-11). Notice God said, "Remember the Sabbath," as it wasn't something new; it had been around since creation. The land also needed to rest (Leviticus 25:4, 8-12). He is very serious, our Lord, about rest.

God desires rest for us because it does not come naturally to us. Why is that? Well, to truly rest we must trust that God will take care of things for us. From the very start in Genesis 3, when we decided that we would make all the decisions and not trust or follow Him, mankind has become more and more stressed and burdened, and less able to relax or find rest. Disobedience started that problem, but obedience will bring to us the rest that God so desires for us to have.

Hebrews 3:7-19 and 4:1-11 both these passages speak on His rest and of warnings about being disobedient and falling short of entering that rest.

71

For Christians, the ultimate rest is found in Christ Jesus. He invites all who are, "weary and burdened" to come to Him and to "cast our cares upon Him" (Matthew 11:28 and 1 Peter 5:7).

For it is only in Him, that we shall find our complete rest. Rest from the cares of this world, from the sorrows that plague us, and from the need to work to make ourselves, "acceptable" to Him.

Jesus is our Sabbath rest.

Only in Him do we have rest in our labors of self effort, because He is holy and righteous.

According to 2 Corinthians 5:21, "God made Him who had no sin to be sin for us, so that in Him we might become the righteousness of God."

We can cease from spiritual, physical, mental, and emotional labors and rest in Him, not just one day a week but always.

Today I am grateful to rest. Like I said, rest does not come easy to me, and today as I have my monthly infusion for treatment of my complex regional pain syndrome (CRPS). I will take advantage of resting my mind, my body, and my spirit in Him. I encourage you to think about the areas that you, too, may need some rest in. Take those things to Jesus today, so that you may have His rest tomorrow.

DAY 27:
A PROFILE OF
COURAGE ...

OCTOBER 29, 2021

Heroes act while others tend to just watch. How many times have you read, seen, or heard of something that turned your spirit to a strong want for justice or to flip the general consensus from what you so strongly believe to be right from wrong? Well, Esther, either by accident of her beauty or accident of the former queen's dismissal, found herself in the role of queen of one of the greatest powers of the world at that time. Then, when all things seemed to be smooth sailing, her crucial moment in time came. It was a time that has been echoed many times since. As a successful racial minority in the Persian Empire, Esther's people, the Jews, had not melted into their surroundings. Many others were jealous of their success and separatism. A vengeful prime minister, Haman, made up his mind to destroy them. He issued an edict of government-sponsored genocide.

Would Esther dare to intervene? Doing so would risk her very life. And what difference could she make? She had become, as queen, a powerless bed partner to a king who strongly preferred women who never interfered with his wishes. She came only when called, and he had not called on her for a month. And yet alone, of all the Jews, she had access to the king.

Her cousin Mordecai reminded her of her very unique place. "Who knows that you have come to such a royal position for such a time as this?" (Esther 4:14). Esther responded with action. Her courageous words are a classic statement of heroism in my heart: "I will go to the king, even though it is against the law. And if I perish, I perish" (Esther 4:16).

This book of Esther clearly shows us, though indirectly, God's heroic concern for His people, the Jews. It runs on a series of extraordinary coincidences. Esther just happened to be chosen as the new queen. The king just happened' to be unable to sleep, and when he picked up some reading, he just happened across an account of a good deed Esther's cousin Mordecai had done. The evil Haman just happened along at that crucial moment. All of these coincidences, happenstances, or God-inky-dinks, as I like to call them, along with Esther's courage, tilted terrible events toward the Jews' favor.

Were these merely all coincidences, or was God behind them? The book does not say directly: God is not mentioned even once, and sometimes seems deliberately left out.

My heartfelt opinion is so the reader can see clearly the faith and the knowing that Esther had inside of her to do what was right. Many times in life we have a deep knowing feeling of right and wrong. Some call it a conscience, others speak of what does your gut tell you. I have come to believe and trust fully in my spirit. I believe this was one of those moments in Esther's life where she just had no doubt of what she was called to do. I also believe Mordecai was an encouraging factor in her decision.

How many times in your life have things come up and you knew what to do but something was stopping you from acting? Then someone speaks about the situation to you and has words of encouragement, reaffirming what you already knew to say or do. Coincidence? I do not believe so. All of life is under God's command. Nothing just happens. These happenings were all part of God's plan to save His people.

As I typed these words to you this morning, God settled my questioning heart, yet again. When I am tired, confused, weary of what I know He wants and expects of me, I ask questions. I have never in my forty-seven years on this earth thought I would write a book, none the less be asked by the Lord to write a book of testimony into my messy life's past, present, and future. Believing and trusting it all to God so faithfully, honestly, and even humbly, getting raw in my feelings and brazen in my expression so others can truly see the Lord's work in and through my fingertips. On these mornings where I start out in question, Why Lord? And in doubt, How Lord? He brings me to a place of coincidence. As I opened up to Esther this morning, I knew already what He wanted me to hear. To read His words again, and to share with you, to maybe be reminded again, or for even the first time, which is beautiful too!

What I am trying to portray to you today is that we need to recognize what He wants of us, and be bold and be confident in it. If there are words to be spoken, ask God for them before you speak. If it's a task to be done, pray to Him asking exactly how to do it. He will guide you. Have no doubts about that my friends.

God protected His people in the book of Esther because he loved them, because He had chosen them from the beginning! And so were you my friend, chosen from the beginning. And maybe this is your time. Maybe all of the brokenness, the chastising, the rebuilding, the refining, and the growth was to place you directly in the position in time where you are, to do precisely what He is calling you to do all along.

Let God be that strength for you. Allow the book of Esther to encourage you, to show how God's exquisite timing—combined with the courage of individuals who happened to be in the right place at the right time—made His chosen people prosper. Imagine what He can do through you and me. He is a God of purpose, in time, space, and life's every circumstance. He is not a God of coincidence, He is a God of purpose. Rest assured of that truth today.

LIVING BY THE SPIRIT AND WALKING INTO FREEDOM

OCTOBER 30, 2021

T he Lord has been speaking to my heart deeply about living by the Spirit. There are two places in the Bible where the phrase "live by the Spirit" spoke to me this morning. In Galatians 5:16, the apostle Paul wrote, "So I say, live by the Spirit, and you will not gratify the desires of the sinful nature." Paul also wrote, in 5:25, "Since we live by the Spirit, let us keep in step with the Spirit."

To live by the Spirit is a given. But to keep in step, actually walk by the Spirit, is not. In other words, we have life by the Holy Spirit, but we do not always obey the Spirit.

In Galatians chapters 1 and 2, Paul insists that he received the gospel directly from God. In addition, he has met every criterion of an apostle. Chapters 3 and 4 deal with Paul's ideas. Had he strayed too far from Old Testament law and customs? Some even hinted that Paul was preaching an incomplete gospel. He answered those objections with a carefully reasoned look at the Old Testament, focusing on Abraham, the father of the Jewish race.

Then Paul turned to more practical matters, stressing freedom, not rules, leaving him open to much criticism. Did his strong emphasis on freedom lead to loose morals? To answer this, he ended Galatians, a letter devoted to Christian liberty, with a warning.

"'Why did Christ set us free?" Paul asks. To make possible a life of orgies, drunkenness, and witchcraft? Obviously not. Christ freed us from worrying about whether we are doing enough to please God and from uselessly following external forms. But we should use that freedom to serve one another in love and to live a Spirit-filled life.

Chapter 6 describes a spirit of tolerance and forgiveness toward those who fail. It also offers encouragement for people who grow tired of doing good when it appears justice is not working out. His arguments and emotions exhausted, Paul concludes, "Neither circumcision nor uncircumcision means anything; what counts is a new creation" (6:15).

A released prisoner, a freed slave, the bountiful fruit of a living tree—all the images Galatians convey to me this morning are life, an abundant life in the Spirit of God, readily available to every Christian. As we listen to the Spirit and obey the guidance given, the freedom we experience in our life now as we step into walking in the Spirit is overwhelming. The confidence in the Spirit given to us releases all doubt, all worry, and sets freedom rapidly evident as we walk in life.

I pray this morning that you feel the Spirit draw you in and that you hear it ever so clearly as you act in obedience today. You have freedom as you walk this life in Christ. You have freedom in His works. As you bear the fruits of your labor and you sow seeds of faith, feel that freedom He so freely gives to you of that deep-rooted confidence in Him. You are no longer who you had been, you are new, free in Christ. The Spirit leads you from the inside, not the world you are living in outside of you. May I encourage you to live and walk in His Spirit today? Your steps will never stumble and your path will remain clear.

DAY 29:
LIKE A RELUCTANT MESSENGER ...

OCTOBER 31, 2021

I woke this morning with a heart so heavy, yearning for my loved ones to hear Him calling them, to recognize their troubles as they are: sin. Wanting and praying for better outcomes and happier spirits. For joy to return in places where it once shone so bright. This is my heartfelt prayer this morning. The Lord drew me to Jeremiah.

Jeremiah 1:7-8, "But the Lord said to me, 'Do not say, "I am only a child." You must go to everyone I send you to and say whatever I command you. Do not be afraid of them, for I am with you and will rescue you,' declares the Lord.

As I read these words today, I feel like no prophet exposed his feelings more than Jeremiah throughout this book. So many roads were taken and travelled in His relationship with God. His relationship with the Lord was streaked with quarrels, reproaches, and outbursts. He told God he wished he were dead (20:14-18).

He accused the Lord of being unreliable (15:18). But the Lord offered him no sympathy. Rather, He promised more of the same, reminding Jeremiah of His promise to stand by him (12:5-6; 15:19-20). Their relationship, doubts and all, forms one of the best examples in the Bible for me, of exactly what it truly means to follow God in spite of everything!

Just like Jeremiah, we fear the unknown, the uncertainties of death. We are weary of ridicule. We hate the discomfort of standing alone against the crowd. And Jeremiah told God exactly how he felt. Yet he obeyed God, and in the end his message proved true. He stood far greater a man than the kings in their palaces who imprisoned him and burned his writings.

He spoke a gloomy message in a gloomy time, and as a result his words are not always pleasant to read. He reminds us, in an era of television smiles and fake happiness, that God's word is not always comforting and encouraging. Those who disregard Him will have reason to fear. For a world that defies Him, He plans judgement, my friends. And no one, not even His chosen messengers, will escape suffering. God's presence will make us strong enough to face it. It is our task to seek it.

Just like Jeremiah, I find myself struggling with insecurities and doubts. I see my loved ones suffer from mistakes made in the flesh and then beat themselves up over them instead of submitting to God in their struggle. I understand that feeling, all too well. As I make my planned schedules and I type these words, I find myself attempting to reason with my father throughout it all. *What am I doing? How can I do this? I can't do this Lord. I am not qualified for this job.*

I believe that we all can relate to those feelings at specific moments where we had to dig in deep to His presence and His will to endure for the task at hand. But the message remains the same!

He wants us to obey Him, His ways, His words, His lead. Believe He has our best interest at heart, for He absolutely does. Knowing it is He that perseveres through us in our forward march on this earth in our flesh we battle daily. Using those triumphs through Him as powerful truths against adversities when they come of what He has already done and will continue to do. We must not be reluctant in our walk. Giving God the glory He so deserves in everything said and done.

Jeremiah 29:11-14, "'For I know the plans I have for you,' declares the Lord, 'plans to prosper you and not harm you, plans to give you hope and a future. Then you will call upon me, and I will listen to you. You will seek me and find me, when you seek me with all your heart. I will be found by you,' declares the Lord, 'and I will bring you back from captivity.'"

How comforting and reassuring it is to believe that He has everything in His plan, knowing in our obedience that He will move mountains and part seas. Have faith in the size of a mustard seed that spreads like deep and vast oceans in depth and size. Rooted, grounded, and steadfast in the knowing of our God.

Galatians 42:6, "Whether it is favorable or unfavorable, we will obey the Lord our God, to whom we are sending you, so that it will go well with us, for we will obey the Lord our God."

DAY 30:
NEW BEGINNINGS ...

NOVEMBER 1, 2021

E zra 3:11, With praise and thanksgiving they sang to the Lord, "He is good: his love to Israel endures forever." And all the people gave a great shout of praise to the Lord, because the foundation of the house of the Lord was laid.

Today as I begin to soak deeply in His word and type these words to you, I am drawn to the book of Ezra. Chapter 4 was where I felt led to read. All of the opposition to the rebuilding! I heard His soft whisper to go back to the beginning, and as I read through from chapters 1 through 10, I recognize that so much has been discussed between my Father and I these last thirty days. Reminders on the way, repentance to be sought was given grace, strongholds set free, lies set apart from truths, work was accomplished when weary, praises and thanksgiving sung, and a fresh start to begin again each morning He wakes me.

Ezra began with exiles. Exiles returning to a ruined city. They had not forgotten. They treasured their spiritual heritage more than the houses and businesses they had built. They wanted to live and worship God in the place God had given His people. Any sacrifice was worth this opportunity. Their first impulse was to rebuild the temple, God's home.

I am reminded about the beginning of this walk, my friends. As I set out to write this book and went my own way, He ever-so-graciously pulled me back into His route instead. God had opened the path for me, but it was my commitment and faithful determination which was needed to follow it.

Once started, opposition seemed to be around every corner. Sometimes it felt close to home, just like the exiles. The work done (my way), all my writings were at a sit still. Here came God's second push, not just to the exiles in Ezra but for me too! This second (push) is described in chapters 5-6. When opposition arose this time, the Israelites managed to push through again, with the assistance of a Persian king. My king has been the faithful friends and family around me. Encouraging, supporting, and praying.

And then another problem preoccupies the last four chapters. Now, Ezra, the man after whom the book is named, actually arrived in Jerusalem during this period, eighty years after the first party.

The temple had been up for half a century. But the new beginning stood in severe jeopardy again. You see, the Israelites began to mingle and compromise their faith with the hostile people around them. Ezra's leadership, which came from a deep biblical faith and genuine sorrow over sin, forced a radical and a painful solution.

The book of Ezra introduces an entirely new period in Israel's history, a period in which they became more like a church than a nation. They became the body of Christ and not just an army of recourse.

Friends, I would like to take this opportunity to share what He is speaking to my heart right now. Just like the book of Ezra, I heard the task, I started strong and full of ambition. I stumbled, and got off track. But His persistence to rebuild and restart was always just a gentle push to keep the pace of work up. He showed me that I didn't need to become an army. I didn't need to be as hard and as strict in my ways, I just needed to follow His lead and the church body lifted me when I struggled. The church and the love of it held me in intercession at times when I couldn't pray for myself. The church held me accountable in my work. For the seasons I felt alone, my church reminded me that, in this new beginning, I was not. In the beginning, I was so focused on fighting the oppositions that may or may not arise, but now, thirty days later in this walk, I am focused on fighting the sin and the spiritual compromise that has tried to elude me, to keep me unsuccessful for God and stagnant in my walk.

Sometimes the fear of starting again is scary enough to stop us in our tracks. When you've done so much work and it all gets set aside or maybe deleted from existence. Where do I start? What do I say now? I'm confused. I'm lost. I'm scared and worried.

As soon as I have recognized those taunts of the enemy and submit to my Father, then I hear His voice saying, *It's a new day to begin again.* I am forever grateful for His pushes and His rests in this time. I am grateful to grow in this process and share His work in me and through me with you.

Is there an area in yourself that you feel Him pushing you to change? Maybe something that no longer serves you? Something holding you back from moving forward? Heed His push, my friend. I pray this encourages you to read the book of Ezra and feel His push for you today. Start new, begin again, and follow the path that leads to Jesus. You will see Him do the biggest of things, in the simplest of ways and in the shortest of times, through just submission. Though the process may be painful, the lessons learned will be rich and the reward is beyond what you ever imagined possible.

Thank you for taking this walk with me and the Lord. My hope is that you have been blessed as sweetly as I have been and a fire has been sparked to grow deep in your spirit. May God bless each step you take in your walk now. This is the time.

ABOUT THE AUTHOR:

A t the age of seventeen, I met Jesus. I am now forty-eight. I have been married 25 years and we have 3 daughters as well as currently 2 grand-children. During the past thirty years of walking with the Lord, He has rescued me from many years of worldly advice and treatments for anxiety, depression, bipolar disorder, and CRPS, where many medications had me trapped in a reliance on doctors for my life. At one of the darkest and lowest seasons, I began to journal. I also started to read a devotional when I found nothing that could help my weakened state of longing for the pain to just cease in my life of endless struggle, as I found myself yet again in a hospital for my mental health and later for my physical health. It was that simple devotional that encouraged me to read my bible again, pray again, and, I can honestly say, led me back to God, and my relationship with Him soared to an entirely different level of intimacy and to a recognition of the lessons He had allowed me to face and overcome as to use me just as He saw fit to help others struggling in their journey with Him, too.

I had to spend a few dark seasons in my walk thus far, to teach me and to mold me in many areas He required of me to change and some to leave behind completely. The good Lord provided me with strength and a deep faith as I walked through trials and illnesses. I pray that this book helps women that may find themselves discouraged and even lost—in maybe a hard season or a critical circumstance—to open their hearts and minds to the truths of the Lord's mercy and grace, that His love is felt and they desire to have a more personal and deeper relationship with God as they walk along their road with Him too. We all need Jesus in this day and time, and I am so grateful to share my walk alongside Him with you.